PASSOVER SEDER FOR CHRISTIAN SUNDAY SCHOOL & FAMILY

Passover is one of the most important events of the Bible. Jesus celebrated the Passover with His disciples the night before he was crucified. "Behold the lamb of God which taketh away the sins of the world." John 1:29. The Jews and the gentiles understand this statement. Since the Garden of Eden a lamb sacrifice was used to cover the sins of man-this lamb, Jesus, was sufficient to take away all the sins of the world. That was a mighty testimony, a Messiah they had been waiting for. The revelation of the deliverance from the kingdom of darkness (Egypt, the world) into the kingdom of light, the family of God, is so poignant in this celebration. The types and shadows of the coming Messiah, Jesus Christ, the lamb of God whose blood is shed is symbolically represented by the blood of the Passover lamb and placed on the doorposts forming a cross. By the end of the Seder the students have come into a deeper relationship with Jesus Christ, a holy and anointed visit. By the third cup they have a clear revelation of communion, which will stay with them each time they take communion. I have seen the entire Sunday School class sit under the presence of the Holy Ghost, not moving, not speaking, as He ministered to them at the end of this Passover Sunday School lesson.

May it bless you.

Blessings!

Joan Ottulich

Copyright © 2017 by Joan Ottulich
All Right Reserved
ISBN-10: 1542563224
ISBN-13: 978-1542563222

MATERIALS NEEDED-PASSOVER SEDAR FOR GENTILE SUNDAY SCHOOL STUDENTS

- Bible
- Wooden spoon or dust pan
- Feather or brush for brushing up crumbs
- White table cloth (disposable)
- Small white paper plates.
- Small, white paper cups.-2each
- White plastic spoons, forks and knives.
- White napkins
- Two white candles.
- White serving dishes.
- Charoset-mixture of apples, raisins, nuts- applesauce or dried apples, raisins, nuts for the sweet.
- Lamb-small amount for a taste only.
- Eggs.
- Parsley
- Salted water
- Grape juice
- Matzah crackers
- Large (6') doorway size piece of paper with picture of Jesus holding a lamb either drawn or taped on.
- Bucket of water with red food color in water.
- Hyssop branch made of either a dried weed with whitish fluff (found in spring from winter) or stick with cotton attached.

Passover Seder for Gentile Sunday School Students & Family

(Most of this is to be read to the students except for instruction areas designated by an *)

The Passover ordinance was given to the Chosen People, the Jews, by God, in the wilderness during their flight from Egypt. It is also known as Pesach (pay-sac) and 'The Festival of Freedom', which begins on the 14th of Nissan, the first month of the Jewish calendar coinciding with the first full moon. Passover celebrates that the blood of the lamb (the last plague upon the Egyptians Ex.11:1) was to be put upon the doorposts and the upper door so that the death angel would 'pass over' their homes when the angel passed over Egypt. All homes 'covered by the blood' were not affected but all homes not covered by the blood, (the Egyptians) suffered the loss of their first born child (Exodus 12). The blood of the lamb is symbolic of the blood of the 'Lamb of God', Jesus, whose blood was shed upon the cross (which can also symbolize the doorposts and upper door), for the salvation of the world. God the Father instituted this festival that the deliverance would be remembered throughout generations to the Jewish people, as well as to the gentile believers that would enter into the covenant. It is a powerful witnessing tool to the Jewish people of what Jesus Christ has done for them.

People traveled from long distances to be in Jerusalem to celebrate the festivals. Jesus and his disciples traveled from Galilee, many miles away, to celebrate Passover. The Passover was celebrated by Jesus and his disciples the night before His crucifixion, and today we will find out why. None of the things we will learn do the Jewish people understand; they perform a festival filled with ritual and enjoy it, but do not have the full meaning because they do not know Jesus their Messiah.

Jesus suffered many hardships in traveling to these feasts. There was, in certain terms, a price on Jesus head (Zola Levitt) and He would often travel in secret. Even His brothers taunted Him about attending the Feast of Tabernacles saying, "Depart hence, and go into Judea, that thy disciples also may see the works that thou doest. For there is no man that doeth anything in secret, and he himself seeketh to be known openly. If thou do these things, shew thyself to the world. For neither did his brethren believe in Him. Then Jesus said unto them, "My time is not yet come." This meant He knew they sought to kill Him and because He did only what the Father told him, He would not be taunted into making a move that the Father was not telling Him to make. Sometimes the Father says do not do that or go there yet. He knew it was getting closer to the time for Him to be arrested and if He went He might be arrested before He had done everything He was supposed to do, such as Passover with the disciples.

What did Passover celebrate? For the Jewish people it was a celebration of remembering the night they were taken out of a dark place, Egypt; while this is all true, it is symbolic of salvation, the deliverance of man out of the kingdom of darkness into the kingdom of His dear Son.

PURGING OUT THE LEAVEN

The house must be cleaned to the point of being sterilized in celebration of this grand occasion. Every family member takes part in this special housecleaning. In particular, the house must be free of all leaven. What is leaven? Leaven is mostly thought of as what makes bread rise. In spiritual thinking it is thought of as sin that grows and grows and takes over to destroy a person. The Bible says, "then when lust hath conceived (or when we act upon a strong desire that we know is not right), it bringeth forth sin: and sin, when sin is finished, bringeth forth death" (James 1:14). In the Jewish family during Passover the father initiates a game with the children, hiding crumbs of bread, which are swept up with a feather into a wooden spoon and then thrown into the fire, sweeping up and burning all the past sins and bad works. 1Cor. 5: 7-8. "Purge out therefore the old leaven, that ye may be a new lump, as ye are unleavened. For even Christ our Passover is sacrificed for us: Therefore, let us keep the feast, not with the old leaven, neither with the leaven of malice and wickedness; but with the unleavened bread of sincerity and truth." This is a picture of being made pure.

*Tell the students to find bread crumbs in clusters under chairs and other places, and brush them into a wooden spoon. We then put them in a designated box or bag, which will be the fire.

Continue reading-

"For the fine (white) linen is the Righteousness of the Saints".

Rev. 19: 8-9 And to her it was granted that she should be arrayed in fine linen, clean and white: for the fine linen is the righteousness of the Saints. And He saith unto me: Write, Blessed are they which are called unto the marriage supper of the Lamb. And He saith unto me, these are the true sayings of God.

*Point to the table to indicate the symbolic representation of the 'fine linen'-the Righteousness of the Saints.

*Have the table set with a white tablecloth, white napkins, white paper cups-3 for each, one to drink from and one that stays empty, and one with salted water, small white paper plates (two each), white utensils, white candles (I use a white paper table cloth and plastic items to dispose of afterwards). I have the table completely set with the foods, grape drink for wine, lamb, small paper cups of saltwater with a sprig of parsley by it for each person for the bitter herb, charoset (mixture of apples, nuts, spices and honey for the sweet-there are different recipes or applesauce can be used. I have even used a dish of dried fruits, apple, raisins and nuts), boiled eggs (I have made deviled eggs and even jello eggs for fun) and horseradish. Matzah crackers are needed, but not on the table, set aside. If possible use a low table with cushions to recline on the floor. A cloth or bag that can be folded to form 3 compartments, each holds a whole matzah cracker. Under one plate place a nickel or quarter (which is thinner). If the student finds it tell him/her to put it back and it will be explained later. An extra chair at the table with a place setting; after all students have arrived either remove extra settings or place more as the case may be, but leave the one empty seat and setting or add as needed.

Continue reading-The mother of the house lights the candles. (One of the female students lights the candles). This is one of the few things a Jewish woman is allowed to do in the Jewish religion. Men and women are kept separate in worship. At the "Wailing Wall" there is a place for men and a smaller place at the other end for women (*explain the Wailing Wall) **Continue reading**-the original wall of protection built of stone around Jerusalem where Jewish people go for intense praying and to place prayer requests written on paper into the cracks on the wall. The woman lighting the candles is symbolic of the woman, Mary, whom God called to bring the "light" into the world, Jesus.

*Have one of the students light the candles.-two candles are enough. Pour the first cup. There are four cups in the ceremony.

THE FIRST CUP: THE CUP OF SANCTIFICATION.

This cup sanctifies the table and all the preparations. The father will perform these services (*the teacher takes his place). He gives the table his blessing with his prayer.

We start by saying "Kadesh" which means sanctified -set apart or made Holy.

"Blessed are You, Adonai our God, King of the Universe who chose us from all the peoples and exalted us from all the tongues, and sanctified us with His commandments. And You gave us, Lord our God, with love, appointed times for gladness, festivals, and times of joy, the day of this festival of Matzah (the unleavened bread, without sin), the time of our freedom, a Holy convocation, a memorial of the Exodus from Egypt. For you chose us and sanctified us from all the nations and the festivals of Holiness in gladness and joy you gave us a heritage. Blessed are you Adonai, who sanctifies Israel and the seasons.

We drink the first cup.

THE HIDDEN BREAD

*Show the students the 'envelope' with the three compartments holding the Matzah. **Tell them**-The Jewish people thought this must represent Abraham, Isaac and Jacob (*pointing to each section), but it actually represents The Father, Son, and Holy

Ghost. *Remove the center Matzah, which is Jesus. **Show them and tell them** that a Matzah has 'stripes' and is 'pierced'. **Tell them**-I do not believe these stripes and piercings are for no reason but that this spiritually represents Jesus who "hath borne our sorrows: yet we did esteem him stricken, smitten of God and afflicted. But he was wounded for our transgressions, bruised for our iniquities: the chastisement of our peace was upon him and with his stripes we are healed" (Isaiah 53:4-5) and again "They shall look upon me whom they have pierced" Zechariah 12: 10. Explain: Remember they pierced His feet and his hands, as well His side when he was on the cross.

*Then take the middle matzah which you have removed, wrap it in a white cloth and bury it beneath a cushion or other item designated for "burying it" and **explain-** All this is part of what happens at Passover. One Jewish man stated " I always wondered why we buried poor Isaac, but in actuality this represents Jesus, the Son, being buried in the tomb (Zola Levitt).

THE FOUR QUESTIONS

*Pass out the four questions to four students written on a piece of paper and let them read one at a time:

1. Why is this night distinguished from all other nights? On this night we only eat unleavened bread.
2. On all other nights we eat any kinds of herbs, but on this night only bitter herbs. Why?

3. On all other nights we do not dip, but tonight we dip twice. Why?
4. On this night we all recline in our chairs at the table. Why?

THE HAGGADAH-THE PASSOVER BOOK

At this point, the father recites the entire Haggadah book. We for our purposes will summarize: *Point to the items on the table as we talk about them.

This night we remember the Exodus, all the events of the Exodus and how great was the event in which the Lord led his people out of Egypt. The unleavened bread, as we stated in the beginning, represents that we are in a state of remembering and removing sin from before a Holy God.

The bitter herbs remind us of the slavery in Egypt. The salt water reminds us of the tears of slavery and the crossing of the Red Sea. As well the dipping represents our baptism into the death of Jesus Christ; we die to ourselves, our own life, and are raised again in newness of life, the New Birth. Jn 3:3 Except a man be born again, he cannot see the kingdom of God.

*At this point, students are instructed to pick up the parsley. **Say**-this is the bitter herb, dip it in the salt water, the first time is for the tears and for the crossing of the Israelite children across the Red Sea. Dip again; the second is for Pharaoh trying to cross, now down the drink with Pharaoh and swallow it.

*(At this point, most do not want to swallow it, but I do, and tell them it is okay to just put it back in the cup).

On this night we recline rather than stand, as we are no longer slaves but free people. (*If we cannot sit at a low table reclining explain that we are sitting and not standing symbolic of being free but explain that reclining is usually done).
Continue reading-Free not only from the slavery of Pharaoh as the Jewish Passover celebrates but free men and women in Jesus Christ. We are free from the sin nature, free from the kingdom of darkness, Satan's hold, freed by receiving the work Jesus completed on the cross, the death and resurrection of Jesus Christ. We have been transferred from the kingdom of darkness into the Kingdom of God's dear Son.

THE EXODUS

* At this time I have either drawn on a 6' piece of meat wrapping paper or some other large sheet of paper an almost life-size drawing of Jesus holding a lamb or a picture of Jesus holding a lamb placed in the upper center of the paper. I then tape this to a doorway and place a container of water dyed with red food coloring large enough to dip a 'hyssop branch' into, or any long plant branch ending in some white flower or leaf, artificial does not work well but a weed by the roadside does. One can take a branch and glue a cotton ball to it for a hyssop look. I place paper on the floor to catch any dripping water. We begin the teaching of the last plague that caused Pharaoh to release the Israelites from of Egypt.

Read: Exodus 12: 17-39 and Exodus 14: 5-31

*At this point, I have the students, one at a time, take the hyssop (the dried or cotton plant), dip it in the dyed water and touch the top of the paper and the side posts. After all have covered the door with the blood of Jesus, I point out to them that the blood has formed a cross. This is all symbolic of Jesus's blood poured out for us upon the cross. The blood saves.

THE MEAL

*Now we serve the meal: No one eats until all is ready. **First explain**: We are celebrating the same meal that Jesus partook of the night before he was crucified, the Passover meal, referred to as 'The Last Supper.' A very specific important meal and here is why.

*Dish out to each and read:

A little **CHAROSET** (haroset) a mixture made with apples and nuts to celebrate the sweetness of being free, no longer slaves, born again, no longer slaves to sin. The **LAMB**; whose blood was upon the door on the night of the Exodus; but also Jesus was Himself the lamb of God, the final sacrifice about to be offered on the Cross, whose blood, like the lamb's on the three places of the door, would flow on the cross to wash our sins away and whomsoever would receive it. The

HORSERADISH: Is another remembrance of the bitterness of slavery in Egypt, the mortar to make bricks, eaten on a small piece of Matzah. The **BOILED EGG**; this is believed to probably be an addition not originally in the Jewish Passover due to pagan celebration of Ishtar (Easter) but as Christians we know that an egg represents newness of life. God can use all things for good. Easter is better called "First Fruits" another Jewish name for this festival, as it celebrates the firstborn, saved by the blood while the Egyptian firstborn were lost. Jesus was the firstborn from the dead and the beginning of the first fruits of the born again Christian.

*The students may sample the foods. Give them Matzah for the horseradish. Most do not have matured tastes buds and are not interested in anything they are uncertain of such as Charoset or lamb but will eat the egg. It's okay.

THE SECOND CUP: THE CUP OF DELIVERANCE

*A second small cup of juice is poured for the students. With this they pour by drops onto the extra plate and with each drop naming a plague of Israel. **Explain**- before the final plague of the death of the firstborn of the Egyptians, God sent 9 other plagues to help convince Pharaoh to let His people go.

Remember, the plagues only happened to the Egyptians. The Israelites were separated from the Egyptians and lived in a nearby place called Goshen which was not touched by these plagues.

1. The plague of blood-Moses stretched out his staff and the waters of the Nile turned to blood, the fish died and the river stank. Because Pharaohs magicians could also turn the water to blood (battle between Satan and God actually), Pharaoh hardened his heart.
2. The plague of frogs-Moses stretched forth his staff and the frogs came forth from the Nile and filled every place in Egypt even coming upon their bodies, their food, their bedrooms, there were so many. They were piled in heaps and they stank. The magicians were able to bring frogs upon the earth and Pharaoh hardened his heart.
3. The plague of lice-Pharaoh hardened his heart and God told Moses to strike the ground with his staff and lice came forth and filled the earth. At this point, the magicians could no longer bring forth anything that God told Moses to cause to happen. The magicians told Pharaoh "this is the finger of God", they could not do it, but Pharaoh did not repent.

4. The plague of flies-After this Pharaoh still hardened his heart and flies were sent to fill Egypt; they were covered with flies and could not shoo them away.
5. The plague of the death of work animals-The next plague the Lord sent was that the cattle, horses, donkeys and camels in Egypt became sick and died; Pharaoh noticed this did not happen to the Israelites animals. He still hardened his heart.
6. The plague of boils-The Lord told Moses to take handfuls of soot from the furnace and toss it in the air before Pharaoh. Moses did this and the land was filled with the dust of the soot which turned to boils on the flesh of Pharaoh and all the Egyptians and their animals, but not on the Israelites. Boils are like the bubble one gets from a burn. They are filled with liquid and when they burst they are painful.
7. The plague of hail-The Lord told Moses to tell Pharaoh to repent or He would send the worst hail storm (balls of frozen, very hard ice) that ever happened. The Lord warned that anyone or any animals outside would be killed by these very large and hard hailstones. Large hailstones fell that killed animals and people in the fields and destroyed crops.

Pharaoh almost repented but changed his mind. We too must remember to be careful that we do not harden our hearts when the Lord is telling us to change something about ourselves.

8. The plague of locusts-The Lord instructed Moses to ask Pharaoh how long would he refuse to do what God asked of him? If he still continued to refuse to let the Israelites go He would then send locust (grasshoppers) which would devour that which the hail had left including every tree left standing. Pharaoh hardened his heart. Locusts devoured everything in and out of the house. The Lord always gave warning; it was not His desire that any people suffer.
9. The plague of darkness-Moses stretched out his hand at the Lord's command and a thick darkness covered the earth, so thick it could be felt blanketing the Egyptians; but in the land of Goshen there was light. No one in Egypt could move from their spot. A darkness darker than any you have known lay over Egypt for three days that immobilized the people-symbolic of deep sin that separates from God.
10. The plague of the Firstborn-"and the Lord said to Moses at midnight I will go throughout the land of Egypt. Every

firstborn shall die from the firstborn of Pharaoh to the firstborn of female slave to the first born of every animal; but in the land of Goshen it shall not be so". The Lord warned Pharaoh before it happened but he would not listen.

THE THIRD CUP: THE CUP OF REDEMPTION

*We now bring out the buried matzah wrapped in white cloth. **Say**-this piece of unleavened bread must be redeemed. The father usually redeems it for a nickel or some sum; look under your plates, one of you have the nickel with which we will redeem this loaf (*the student then brings forth the nickel and gives it to the teacher). What does it mean to be redeemed? It means to be bought back with a price, liberated. The Israelites were redeemed from the slavery of Egypt, but this act is symbolic of much more. Jesus bought us back from the kingdom of darkness (Satan) who had gained control of us through the fall of Adam into the kingdom of His dear Son, the kingdom of Heaven. God is promising Israel that through everything they shall be ransomed back by the Messiah; the work of Jesus on the cross.

Tell the children-You are now in the upper room with Jesus at the last supper (*a spiritual comparison happens as the students are seated as most photos depict the last supper). *The father (teacher) breaks the matzah into pieces onto a plate and fills the cups with the juice. Have each take a piece of bread and tell them to wait, fill their cups with drink. Tell them to wait to eat and drink.

Say-The father then says a blessing over the bread. Jesus also said the blessing. Every head bowed, every eye closed, I will say it now. "Blessed are Thou, O Lord our God, King of the universe, Who bringest forth bread from the earth."

Say-remember this is the 'Last Supper' the one that Jesus celebrated. He is with us now. He did this same thing at the 'Last Supper'; after they had eaten, he took the bread and broke it and gave to each. He said the blessing, but also said, "Take eat, this is my body which is given for you: this do in remembrance of me. (Luke 22:19)

*Tell them to eat if they haven't. **Say**-Jesus said, "I am the bread of life" John 6:35. With this he was telling them that as the Father brings forth bread from the earth, so Jesus would rise from the dead. His crucified body bought back yours, not only in the life to come but in this life to have victory in every area; He wants you to remember these things.

Then He took the cup and gave the Hebrew blessing.

Every eye closed, every head bowed. Before we take the cup, now is the time to think about how we have been living. If there have been any times you know are not quite right, maybe being unkind or selfish for example, to yourself and to the your Father in heaven ask forgiveness now; for as we take the cup we remember that his blood was shed to wash away our sins. **Say the blessing**-"Blessed art thou, O Lord our God, King of the universe, Creator of the fruit of the vine". Then Jesus took the cup saying, "This is my blood of the New Testament, which is shed for many for the remission of sins. Do ye, as oft as you drink it in remembrance of me. For as oft as you eat this bread, and drink this cup, you do shew the Lord's death til he come. (1 Cor:11: 23-26 & Matt. 26:26-27)

*Tell them to drink the cup.

THE FOURTH CUP: THE CUP OF RESTORATION OR ELIJAH'S CUP

*Point to the empty cup on the table and the empty chair. **Tell them**-In the Jewish Passover, they believe that the empty fourth cup may be awaiting the arrival of the prophet Elijah who will announce, "The waiting is over, the Messiah has come" and Israel will be redeemed. That is why there is an empty place set. *Have one of the students run to the door to see if Elijah is coming. **Tell them**- They do not drink this cup until Elijah arrives and announces the Messiah has come, but Jesus said, "But I say unto you, I will not drink henceforth of this fruit of the vine, until that day when I drink it new with you in my Father's kingdom" (Matthew 26:29). The fourth cup we will drink with Jesus at the marriage supper of the lamb; He is the groom, the believers and New Jerusalem make up the bride and He will have a celebration dinner when all things have come to their end as we know it and Jesus is Lord of all.

Say-and when they had sung an hymn, they went out..
*Sing something they would surely know. Jesus loves me or some hymn of your fellowship.

In this lesson they not only come to understand the Jewish Passover, but they understand how the Old Testament is full of symbols and shadows all about Jesus. They also come to understand the strength of communion which they will carry with them for the rest of their lives.

REFERENCES:

Dake, Finis Jenning..Dake's Annotated Reference Bible. Dake Bible Sales, Inc. Georgia:Lawrence, 16th printing, 1984.

Levit, Zola. The Miracle of Passover. Dallas: Tx Great Impressions Printing & Graphics

NOTES

NOTES